SPACE-LICIOUS! Out-of-This-World Recipes

CREATE!

STARS

SPACE-THEMED RECIPES

by Jane Yates

BEARPORT PUBLISHING

Minneapolis, Minnesota

Credits

Cover and title page, © Anna Kucherova/Adobe Stock and © supamas/Adobe Stock and © sommai/Adobe Stock and © Baurzhan/Adobe Stock and © Nazarii_Neshcherenskyi/Shutterstock; Background images, PaulPaladin/Adobe Stock; Lifestyle Graphic/Adobe Stock; 5 top left, DestinaDesign/Shutterstock.com; 5 right middle,prasith/Adobe Stock; 6 bottom left, kotoffei/Adobe Stock; 6 bottom right, Till Credner/Creative Commons; 10, © Sunflower/Adobe Stock; 14 bottom left, NASA, ESA, CSA, STScI, Webb ERO Production Team / Public Domain; 16 bottom left, Siberian Art/Shutterstock.com; 16 bottom right, Wiaskara/Creative Commons; 18 bottom right, Nazarii_Neshcherenskyi/Shutterstock.com; 22 top right, NASA/Public Domain; all other photos ©Austen Photography

Bearport Publishing Company Product Development Team

Publisher: Jen Jenson; Director of Product Development: Spencer Brinker; Editorial Director: Allison Juda; Editor: Cole Nelson; Editor: Tiana Tran; Production Editor: Naomi Reich; Art Director: Kim Jones; Designer: Kayla Eggert; Designer: Steve Scheluchin; Production Specialist: Owen Hamlin

Statement on Usage of Generative Artificial Intelligence

Bearport Publishing remains committed to publishing high-quality nonfiction books. Therefore, we restrict the use of generative AI to ensure accuracy of all text and visual components pertaining to a book's subject. See BearportPublishing.com for details.

Produced for Bearport Publishing by BlueAppleWorks Inc.

Managing Editor for BlueAppleWorks: Melissa McClellan
Art Director: T.J. Choleva
Photo Research: Jane Reid

Library of Congress Cataloging-in-Publication Data

Names: Yates, Jane, author.
Title: Stars : space-themed recipes / by Jane Yates.
Description: Minneapolis, Minnesota : Bearport Publishing Company, [2026] |
  Series: Space-licious! out-of-this-world recipes | Includes
  bibliographical references and index.
Identifiers: LCCN 2025001586 (print) | LCCN 2025001587 (ebook) | ISBN
  9798895770351 (library binding) | ISBN 9798895771525 (ebook)
Subjects: LCSH: Cooking--Juvenile literature. |
  Stars--Miscellanea--Juvenile literature. | Outer
  space--Miscellanea--Juvenile literature. | LCGFT: Cookbooks.
Classification: LCC TX652.5 .Y376 2026 (print) | LCC TX652.5 (ebook) |
  DDC 641.5--dc23/eng/20250227
LC record available at https://lccn.loc.gov/2025001586
LC ebook record available at https://lccn.loc.gov/2025001587

Copyright © 2026 Bearport Publishing Company. All rights reserved. No part of this publication may be reproduced in whole or in part, stored in any retrieval system, or transmitted in any form or by any means, electronic, mechanical, photocopying, recording, or otherwise, without written permission from the publisher. Bearport Publishing is a division of FlutterBee Education Group.

For more information, write to Bearport Publishing, 3500 American Blvd W, Suite 150, Bloomington, MN 55431.

CONTENTS

Space-licious! 4
Cheesy Array 6
Stellar Apples 8
Grilled Yellow Sun 10
Starburst Pickles 14
Sparkling Sunrise 16
Red Giant and
   White Dwarf Cookies 18

Meet a Hungry Astronaut 22
Glossary 23
Index 24
Read More 24
Learn More Online 24
About the Author 24

SPACE-LICIOUS!

Let's learn about space and cooking at the same time! How would you like to try a cheesy grilled sun or some stellar apples? With this book, you can make six delicious, out-of-this-world recipes. Let's blast off!

Measuring liquid ingredients

- Use a measuring cup with a spout. This makes it easier to pour the liquids without spilling.
- Always set the measuring cup on a flat surface.
- When adding liquid, bend down so your eye is level with the measurements on the cup. This ensures you have the right amount.

Measuring dry ingredients

- Scoop the ingredients with the correct size measuring cup or measuring spoon.
- Level off the top with the back of a butter knife or another straight edge. This will ensure you have an accurate amount.

Ingredients

Most of these recipes can be made with things you probably already have in your kitchen. Before you start each recipe, make sure you have all the ingredients you need. It's a good idea to set everything on the counter before you begin.

Microwave safety

Each microwave works a little differently, so ask an adult to help show you how to use yours. Be sure to use only dishes that are safe for the microwave, such as glass or ceramic. Never use metal or aluminum foil in the microwave. After cooking, carefully check that a dish isn't too hot before taking it out.

Allergy Alert!

Recipes that include common allergens, such as wheat, peanuts, eggs, or dairy are marked with a special symbol. Please use a safe **substitute** ingredient if you need to.

 Wheat   Eggs

 Dairy   Peanuts

 Always ask for an adult's help with knives and when using the oven or stove.

CHEESY ARRAY

Throughout history, people have seen and given names to patterns in groups of stars called constellations. Turn the night sky into a delicious treat by creating your own constellation using cheese and pretzels. Try making one of the 12 constellations of the **zodiac**, or design your own!

Ingredients

* 1 slice cheddar cheese
* Pretzel sticks

Allergy Alert!

Equipment

* A cutting board
* A small, star-shaped cookie cutter

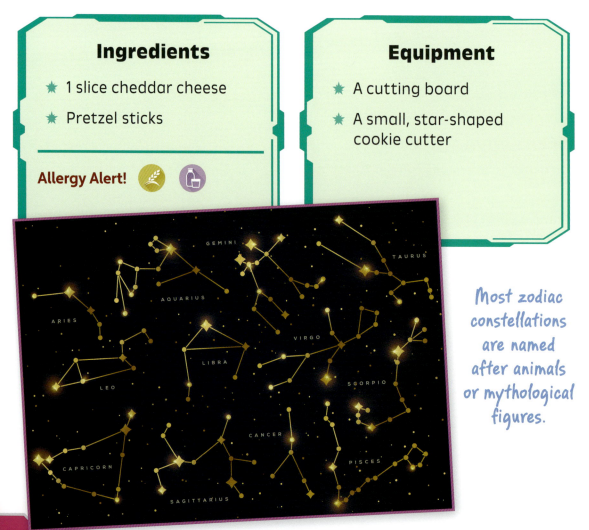

Most zodiac constellations are named after animals or mythological figures.

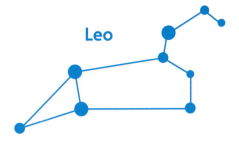

Leo

1. Pick a constellation to use as your guide. For example, you could make the Leo constellation.

2. Lay a piece of cheese on a cutting board. Position a small star-shaped cookie cutter on the cheese, and press down firmly.

3. Remove the cheese star from the cookie cutter and set aside. Continue cutting out stars until you have enough for your constellation.

4. Next, lay out the pretzel sticks to build the shape of the constellation. Break the pretzels into pieces to get the right lengths.

5. Place the cheese stars on top of the ends of the pretzels and where they meet to represent the stars in the constellation.

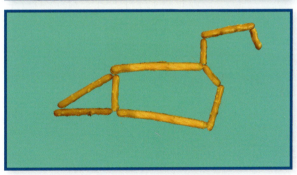

STELLAR APPLES

Stars are giant balls of hot gas. They send out energy from their centers in the form of light and heat. Make your own energy-packed dip to place at the center of this stellar apple star snack.

Ingredients

- 1 apple
- 3 Tbsp yogurt
- 3 Tbsp peanut butter
- 1 Tbsp honey
- 2 Tbsp strawberry jelly

Allergy Alert!

Equipment

- A mixing bowl
- A spoon
- A small dipping bowl
- A cutting board
- An apple cutter
- A plate

1. Wash and dry an apple, set aside.

2. Prepare the dip by scooping the yogurt, peanut butter, and honey into a mixing bowl.

3. Stir the ingredients together with a spoon until well mixed.

4. Transfer the the mixture into a small dipping bowl.

5. Next, place the apple on a cutting board, and ask an adult to use an apple cutter to split it into wedges. Discard the apple core.

6. Place the bowl of peanut butter dip in the center of a plate. Arrange the apple wedges around the dip to look like energy coming out from the center of a star.

7. Finally, spread the strawberry jelly on top of the peanut butter dip to give your dish a starry appearance.

GRILLED YELLOW SUN

The sun is a medium-sized star at the center of our **solar system**. It has been around for more than 4.5 billion years, pulling the planets in circular paths around it. Make a warm, gooey grilled cheese sun sandwich the center of your lunch!

Ingredients

* Frozen french fries
* 2 slices of bread
* 2 slices of cheese
* Butter or margarine

Allergy Alert!

Equipment

* A baking sheet
* Parchment paper
* A cutting board
* A 4-in. (10-cm) round cookie cutter
* A butter knife
* A paper towel
* A plate

Scientists have found more than 3,200 other stars in our galaxy with planets orbiting around them.

10

1. Line a baking sheet with parchment paper and place the frozen french fries on it.

2. With an adult's help, bake the french fries in the oven according to the package directions.

3. While the french fries are cooking, put two slices of bread on a cutting board. Place a round cookie cutter on top of one slice and press down to cut out a circle of bread. Repeat for the other slice.

4. Place two slices of cheese on the cutting board. Use the cookie cutter to cut out two round slices of cheese.

11

5 Put the two slices of bread in a toaster. Toast until they are a nice golden color, and then place them back on the cutting board.

6 Spread margarine or butter on one side of each piece of toast with a butter knife.

7 Place one piece of toast butter side down. Place the pieces of cheese on top of the toast. Add the other slice of toast to the stack, butter side up.

8 Wrap the sandwich in a paper towel, and microwave it for 30 seconds to melt the cheese.

9. After the fries have cooled slightly from the oven, arrange them on a plate in a circular pattern. They will represent the rays of light coming out from the sun.

10. Place the grilled cheese sandwich in the center of the french fries. Enjoy!

STARBURST PICKLES

A starburst is a region of space where many new stars are forming. This activity can last for ten million years or more, which is relatively short in the lifespan of a **galaxy**. Create your own pickled starburst region in a jar!

Ingredients

- 1 cucumber
- 1 tsp salt
- 1 bay leaf
- 5–10 peppercorns
- 1 clove garlic, peeled
- 4 sprigs of fresh dill
- ⅓ cup white, apple cider, or rice vinegar
- ⅓ cup water
- 2 Tbsp honey

Equipment

- A knife for your adult helper
- A cutting board
- A small, star-shaped cookie cutter
- A 10-oz (300-mL) glass jar with lid
- A spoon
- A liquid measuring cup

The Tarantula Nebula has long been a favorite among astronomers for studying the formation of new stars.

14

1. Have an adult cut the cucumber into slices that are ¼ inch (0.6 cm) thick. Lay the cucumber slices out on a cutting board.

2. Use the star-shaped cookie cutter to cut out cucumber stars from the slices.

3. Next, add the salt, bay leaf, peppercorns, and garlic to the jar.

4. Break up the sprigs of dill into smaller pieces. Then, add the dill and cucumber stars to the jar in alternating layers.

5. Mix the vinegar, water, and honey in the measuring cup. Stir until the honey is dissolved.

6. Lastly, pour the vinegar mixture over the cucumbers until the jar is filled. Put the lid on, shake the jar gently, and refrigerate. After 6 hours in the fridge, the cucumbers are pickled and ready to eat. Have a starburst blast!

15

SPARKLING SUNRISE

Earth rotates, or spins, in space. As it does, different parts of the planet face the sun's light at different times. This causes our days and nights. Enjoy a refreshing drink with the same colors that light up the sky during this transition from night to day.

Ingredients

* 1 orange slice or wedge
* ¼ cup orange juice
* Sparkling water
* 1 tsp grenadine

Equipment

* 1 cocktail umbrella pick
* A 10-oz (300-mL) glass
* A spoon

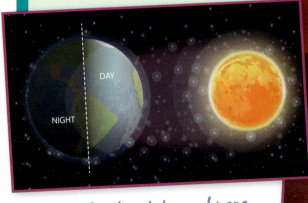

As Earth rotates, only one side of the planet faces the sun at a time. The side facing the sun has daylight.

Earth rotates from west to east. This rotation makes the sun appear to rise in the east and set in the west.

1. Slide the cocktail umbrella pick through the orange slice or wedge and set it aside. This is your **garnish**.

2. Add the orange juice to a glass. Then, fill the glass up with sparkling water.

3. Slip the orange garnish onto the rim of the glass.

4. Carefully pour the grenadine into the glass. Stir gently to mix the grenadine in the bottom of the glass. Be careful not to stir too hard or you will lose the different shades.

RED GIANT AND WHITE DWARF COOKIES

Scientists group stars by their size and temperature, which they determine by the star's color. A red giant is one of the biggest, coolest kinds of stars. On the other end of the **range**, a white dwarf is a small star that burns very hot. Make sugar cookies to represent these two kinds of stars.

Ingredients

For the cookies:
- 1 ½ cups all-purpose flour, plus more for dusting
- ½ tsp baking soda
- ¼ tsp baking powder
- ½ tsp salt
- ½ cup butter, softened
- ¾ cup sugar
- 1 egg
- ½ teaspoon vanilla extract

For the Icing:
- 1 ½ cup powdered sugar
- 3 Tbsp whole milk or cream
- Red food coloring
- Sprinkles

Allergy Alert!

The hottest stars burn blue and white. These are stars that are often approaching the end of their lives.

Equipment

- 4 mixing bowls
- Spoons
- A medium-sized sealable plastic food bag
- A rolling pin
- 2 circle-shaped cookie cutters of different sizes
- Baking sheets
- Parchment paper

Cookies

1. Combine the flour, baking soda, baking powder, and salt in a mixing bowl. Use a spoon to stir, then set aside. These are your dry ingredients.

2. Add the butter to a second mixing bowl. Stir it with a spoon until it becomes creamy.

3. Add the sugar to the butter and stir until well combined.

4. Crack the egg into the bowl. Add the vanilla extract and mix until everything is well blended. These are your wet ingredients.

5. Next, add the dry ingredients to the wet. Stir until the dough is well combined and smooth.

6 Place the dough into a medium-sized plastic food bag. Use a rolling pin to flatten the dough evenly inside the bag, and zip the bag closed. Refrigerate the dough for at least 1 hour.

7 Lightly **dust** your work surface with flour to prevent sticking. Carefully remove the cookie dough from the bag and place it on the floured surface.

8 Use cookie cutters to cut out large and small circles from the dough. Gather any leftover dough, reroll it, and cut out additional circles until the dough is used up.

9 **Preheat** the oven to 350°F (175°C). Line baking sheets with parchment paper, and place the cookies about 1 in. (2.5 cm) apart on the parchment paper.

10 Bake the cookies for 10–14 minutes, or until golden around the edges. Let cool on the baking sheet.

Icing

1. As the cookies cool, start making icing. Pour the powdered sugar into a bowl. Add the milk and stir until well mixed. If your icing is too thick, add several drops of milk and stir. If it's too thin, add a spoonful of powdered sugar, and mix well.

2. Transfer about half of the icing into another bowl.

3. Add a few drops of red food coloring to one bowl and stir. Keep adding food coloring until you achieve the desired color.

4. Place a scoop of red icing on each large cookie. Spread it evenly with a spoon until the cookie is fully covered. Repeat with the white icing on the small cookies.

5. Decorate the cookies with sprinkles.

MEET A HUNGRY ASTRONAUT

NASA astronaut Neil Armstrong was the first person to walk on the moon. There weren't many food options while he was on his journey to and from space. Astronauts had bacon squares, beef stew, and sugar cookie cubes. These cookies had to be eaten in one bite to prevent crumbs, which could harm the electronics on their spacecraft.

Neil ate sugar cookies on the moon!

Make Space-licious Sugar Cookies

1. Make cookie dough using the recipe on pages 18–20, through the step for refrigerating the dough.
2. Roll the dough out into a ½-in. (1.3-cm) slab.
3. Use a butter knife to cut the dough into squares.
4. Place the squares on a parchment paper-lined baking sheet. Bake the cookies for 12 minutes at 350°F (175°C). Decorate with sprinkles.

GLOSSARY

dust to lightly coat a food ingredient or cooking surface with a dry ingredient, such as flour

galaxy a massive collection of stars, planets, gas, and space dust, all held together by gravity

garnish a decorative element added to food or drink

gravity the attracting force between all objects

NASA the National Aeronautics and Space Administration, a United States government agency responsible for space exploration

preheat to heat in advance to a set temperature

range the difference between the highest and lowest values in a set or on a scale

solar system a collection of planets, moons, asteroids, comets, and other objects that orbit a central star

substitute a similar item used in place of another item

zodiac an imaginary belt in the sky that includes the apparent paths of most of the planets and is divided into 12 star groups or signs

INDEX

allergy 5–6, 8, 10, 18
apples 4, 8–9, 14
Armstrong, Neil 22
cheese 6–7, 10–13
constellation 6–7
cookies 18, 20–22
drink 16
pickles 14–15
red giant stars 18
solar system 10
sun 4, 10, 13, 16
white dwarf stars 18

READ MORE

Betts, Bruce. *The Sun: Our Solar System's Star (Exploring Our Solar System with the Planetary Society)*. Minneapolis: Lerner Publications, 2025.

Mather, Charis. *Stars: Top-Secret Data (Space Files)*. Minneapolis: Bearport Publishing, 2024.

LEARN MORE ONLINE

1. Go to **FactSurfer.com** or scan the QR code below.
2. Enter "**Star Recipes**" into the search box.
3. Click on the cover of this book to see a list of websites.

ABOUT THE AUTHOR

Jane Yates is an avid cook who worked in restaurants while attending art school. She has written more than 20 craft books for children.